IMPROVING
VOCABULARY

for ages 8-9

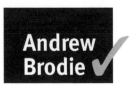

Andrew Brodie

Introduction

All the activities in *Improving Vocabulary* are specifically designed to promote pupils' knowledge and use of an extensive range of words in their speaking and listening, reading and writing. This six book series provides a structured programme of activities, which will ultimately form invaluable practice for the English grammar, punctuation and spelling test at the end of Key Stage 2.

Research has shown that good use of vocabulary is vitally important for learning and that there is a clear link between a child's level of vocabulary at age five and his or her future success at sixteen or beyond. For good educational progress to be made, children need to experience high-quality language development activities.

Throughout the books, the vocabulary has been carefully selected for the designated age group and progression is also integral to the activities. The activity sheets are differentiated at three levels and are designed to be used by individuals or small groups working with an adult. **Teacher's notes** on each sheet provide guidance on how to get the most from the activity. In general, adults should encourage the children to respond to low-demand questions first before moving on to high-demand questions as they become more confident.

How to use the book and CD-ROM together

The revised National Curriculum Programme of Study for Years 3 and 4 indicates the importance of learning new vocabulary, particularly as part of the reading process. The Programme of Study states that 'teachers should continue to emphasise pupils' enjoyment and understanding of language, especially vocabulary, to support their reading and writing'. It also says 'there will continue to be a need for pupils to learn subject-specific vocabulary'. The Programme of Study for Writing states that pupils should be taught to draft and write by 'selecting appropriate grammar and vocabulary, understanding how such choices can change and enhance meaning'. The activities in this book provide opportunities for practising all of these aspects of the National Curriculum, as well as other important language development skills such as word categorisation.

The book has fifteen Key Activities, which can be projected on to a whiteboard for whole class use and photocopied/printed for display. Sharing the Key Activities either on screen or paper provides lots of opportunities for speaking and listening, for decoding words through a phonic approach, for reading and writing, and for satisfaction and enjoyment in shared success.

For each Key Activity there are three vocabulary sheets at different levels to enable you to differentiate across the ability range in your class. An animal picture at the top of the sheet indicates the level: the cat exercises are at the simplest level; the dog exercises are at the next level and the rabbit exercises are at the most advanced level. You may start off by giving some pupils the cat worksheet and then decide, on the basis of their success, to move them on to the dog worksheet. A similar approach could be taken with the dog and rabbit sheets.

The activity sheets are aimed at the following ability levels:
- Cat activity sheets are for pupils who may need **extra help**.
- Dog activity sheets are for pupils who are **progressing well**.
- Rabbit activity sheets are for **higher ability pupils**.

Contents

Journeys

Verbs

Nouns

Adjectives

Teacher's notes

Photocopy and cut out these category title cards to use in conjunction with the activities on the following three sheets. This activity provides lots of opportunities for speaking and listening and introduces important everyday vocabulary.

Journeys

Teacher's notes

Cut out the words and illustrations below and use them in conjunction with the category title cards from page 5. Use the cards created from this sheet as prompts for discussion to ensure that this is a speaking and listening activity as well as a reading task. Encourage the children to talk about journeys they have made. How did they travel? Why were they on the journey? How far was it? How long did it take? Can the children create oral sentences using some of the doing words with some of the describing words and naming words?

bus	car	train	aeroplane	ferry
journey	distant	places	holiday	visiting
relations	relatives	motorway	railway	channel
tunnel	bridge	long	boring	never-ending
travel	North	South	East	West

Andrew Brodie: Improving Vocabulary for ages 8-9 © Bloomsbury Publishing Plc 2012

Journeys

Name _____

Date _____

Teacher's notes

Discuss the words in the Word Bank in conjunction with the category title cards from page 5. Ensure that this is firstly a speaking and listening activity although it will provide practice in both reading and writing. Note the inclusion of the words 'farther' and 'farthest', which are variations of the words 'further' and 'furthest' that tend to be used in regard to physical distance. Encourage the children to talk about journeys they have made. How did they travel? Why were they on the journey? How far was it? How long did it take? Can the children create oral sentences using some of the doing words with some of the describing words and naming words? Once they are confident with the words ask them to write them in the correct section of the table. Finally, they can write two sentences each containing at least one of the verbs, one of the adjectives and one of the nouns.

Word Bank

aeroplane far long distant travelled visiting East never-ending
border farthest motorway train
distance places nearer farther car relatives further
West channel North nearest close
near holiday boring South travel tunnel
direction transport
railway bridge furthest travelling journey ferry
bus relations

Write each of the words from the Word Bank in the correct section of the table.

Nouns	Adjectives	Verbs

Can you think of any extra words to write in the table?
Write two sentences. Use a verb, a noun and an adjective from the table in each one.

_____

_____

_____

_____

Journeys

Name _____

Date _____

Teacher's notes

Discuss the words in the Word Bank in conjunction with the category title cards from page 5. Ensure that this is firstly a speaking and listening activity although it will provide practice in both reading and writing. Note the inclusion of the words 'farther' and 'farthest', which are variations of the words 'further' and 'furthest' that tend to be used in regard to physical distance. Encourage the children to talk about journeys they have made. How did they travel? Why were they on the journey? How far was it? How long did it take? Can the children create oral sentences using some of the doing words with some of the describing words and naming words? Once they are confident with the words ask them to write four well-structured sentences using nouns, verbs and, where appropriate, adjectives all related to journeys.

Word Bank

never-ending   near   aeroplane

distance   ferry   travelling   travel   relations   West

farther   nearer   nearest   close   train

far   East   car   distant   visiting

journey   channel

farthest   tunnel   motorway   furthest   railway

places   travelled   bridge   border   holiday

direction   boring   South

North   long   further   bus

transport   relatives

Can you think of any extra words regarding journeys?
Write four brilliant sentences about journeys.

_____

_____

_____

_____

_____

_____

_____

_____

_____

_____

_____

_____

Andrew Brodie: Improving Vocabulary for ages 8-9 © Bloomsbury Publishing Plc 2012

Group words

Group words

Collective nouns

Teacher's notes

Photocopy and cut out these category title cards to use in conjunction with the activities on the following three sheets.

Group words

Teacher's notes

Cut out the words and illustrations below and check that the children understand that the activity involves the use of group words (collective nouns). Try to ensure that this is a speaking and listening activity as well as a reading task. Encourage the children to think carefully about each of the items shown on the cards, helping them to match the plural items to the appropriate collective nouns. You may also wish to sort them in other ways: for example into living and non-living things. Ask them to compose some oral sentences, which include a collective noun used appropriately. As an extension activity the pupils could write out a sentence, correctly composed and punctuated.

bees	flies	birds	flowers
cows	sheep	cards	elephants
herd	swarm	flock	bunch
pack	host	angels	squad
soldiers	athletes	band	musicians

Group words

Teacher's notes

Encourage the children to talk about the group words (collective nouns) listed in the Word Bank, creating oral sentences using these words appropriately with some of the animals or objects also listed. Talk about when the word 'team' would be used, rather than 'herd', in relation to a group of horses (e.g., when the horses are pulling a carriage). Note that either 'flock' or 'herd' is correct when referring to goats. When they are confident in using the words effectively, they can complete the other activities on the sheet. Note, however, that the emphasis of the work should be on speaking and listening.

Word Bank

bees   flowers   flies   angels   horses

birds   cows   musicians   elephants

sheep   herd   flock   host   squad

wolves   goats   deer

cards   grapes

band   athletes   swarm   pack

team   zebras   bunch   hounds   soldiers

Insert an appropriate collective noun in each of the gaps below.

a _____ of grapes   a _____ of deer   a _____ of bees

a _____ of elephants   a _____ of wolves   a _____ of horses

a _____ of cards   a _____ of sheep   a _____ of horses

a _____ of flowers   a _____ of zebras   a _____ of cows

a _____ of birds   a _____ of flies   a _____ of goats

Write two sentences, each of which contains a collective noun for a group.

_____

_____

_____

_____

Group words

Teacher's notes

Ask the children to talk about the group words (collective nouns) listed in the Word Bank, creating oral sentences using these words appropriately with some of the animals or objects also listed. Note that we are not seeking for children to know and remember all of the collective nouns. Instead, we are trying to encourage them to consider why certain vocabulary may have been chosen. Some of the links between particular collective nouns and particular animals, birds or objects are not obvious, but may be worked out by a process of elimination. When they are confident in using the words effectively, they can complete the other activities on the sheet.

Word Bank

cloud   ants   angels   host   cards   gnats   alligators

gaggle   school   army   cattle   athletes   dogs   band

crows   baboons   soldiers   wolves   pack   bats   dolphins

troop   colony   herd   squad   murder   geese

congregation   musicians

Insert an appropriate collective noun in each of the gaps below.

a _____ of geese   an _____ of ants   a _____ of dogs

a _____ of alligators   a _____ of crows   a _____ of cattle

a _____ of gnats   a _____ of dolphins   a _____ of bats

a _____ of baboons   a _____ of cards   a _____ of wolves

Write two sentences, each of which contains a collective noun for a group.

_____   _____

_____   _____

Can you make up your own collective nouns? Try to think of some ideas for these people or objects:

a _____ of doctors   a _____ of pencils   a _____ of clocks

_____

_____

_____

_____

     Andrew Brodie: Improving Vocabulary for ages 8-9 © Bloomsbury Publishing Plc 2012

Word sorting: human body, bird life, art

Non-fiction

Information

The human body

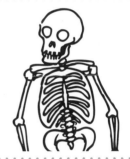

Bird life

Art

Teacher's notes

Photocopy and cut out the Non-fiction or Information headings and the category title cards to use in conjunction with the activities on the following three sheets. This type of categorisation activity can be very challenging for some children. It is important that they explain their choices when they are sorting the words - they may make some surprising decisions but ones that are perfectly valid.

Word sorting:
human body, bird life, art

Teacher's notes

Cut out the words and illustrations below and use them in conjunction with the category title cards from page 13. Ask the children to sort the words as though they appear in some non-fiction books: which words could be found in a book about bird life, which in a book about the human body and which could be found in a book about art? Could any of the words appear in more than one of the books? Could any of the words appear in all three books? As an extension activity, ask the children to compose orally two or three sentences that feature some of the words they have discussed. They could write out the best sentences.

skeleton	habitat	skull	chest	shin
knee-cap	stomach	sculpture	portrait	pattern
collage	viewpoint	painting	head	nest
flight	wings	leg	foot	wing-tips
artist	illustrate	breathing	lungs	heart

Andrew Brodie: Improving Vocabulary for ages 8-9 © Bloomsbury Publishing Plc 2012

Word sorting: human body, bird life, art

Teacher's notes

Discuss the words below in relation to the category title cards from page 13. Do the children know what each word means? Can they think of any related words? For example, they could suggest the word 'identify' in relation to the word 'identification'. Ask the children to sort the words as though they appear in some non-fiction books: Could any of the words appear in more than one of the books? Could any of the words appear in all three books?

Word Bank

skeleton knee-cap stomach sculpture habitat shin head
skull breathing heart painting chest nestlings
portrait lungs flight wings artist nest
pattern collage easel watercolour print-making
viewpoint prey palette hatching
leg feathers thigh artist
foot plumage rib-cage illustrate identification incubate
torso

Look carefully at the words in the Word Bank. Which words could be found in a book about bird life, which in a book about the human body and which could be found in a book about art? Write the words in the correct places below. Some of the words could appear in more than one book.

The Human Body

_____ _____
_____ _____
_____ _____
_____ _____
_____ _____
_____ _____
_____ _____
_____ _____

Bird Life

_____ _____
_____ _____
_____ _____
_____ _____
_____ _____
_____ _____
_____ _____
_____ _____

ART

_____ _____
_____ _____
_____ _____
_____ _____
_____ _____
_____ _____
_____ _____
_____ _____

On a separate piece of paper, write three sentences using some of the vocabulary relating to art, birds or the human body.

Word sorting:
human body, bird life, art

Teacher's notes

Discuss the words below in relation to the category title cards from page 13. Do the children know what each word means? To find extra vocabulary for each list, the children could research in the school library or on the internet. They could also consider searching for words related to those on the list: for example, the word 'incubation' is clearly related to the word 'incubate'.

Word Bank

skeleton   portrait   collage

skull   chest   habitat   stomach   pattern

shin   knee-cap   sculpture   nest

viewpoint   head   leg   feathers

painting   flight   wings

foot   torso   easel   plumage

nestlings   thigh   heart

prey   hatching

artist   illustrate   rib-cage   incubate

artist   watercolour

print-making   palette   lungs   breathing   identification

Look carefully at the words in the Word Bank. Write the words in the correct book below. Some of the words could appear in more than one book.

The Human Body	Bird Life	ART

Find some more vocabulary for each book.

 Andrew Brodie: Improving Vocabulary for ages 8-9 © Bloomsbury Publishing Plc 2012

Word sorting: maths, literacy, history

Non-fiction

Information

Maths

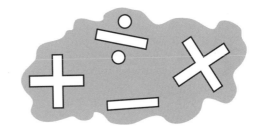

Literacy

History

Teacher's notes

Photocopy and cut out the Non-fiction or Information headings and the category title cards to use in conjunction with the activities on the following three sheets. This type of categorisation activity can be very challenging for some children. It is important that they explain their choices when they are sorting the words - they may make some surprising decisions but ones that are perfectly valid.

Word sorting: maths, literacy, history

Teacher's notes

Cut out the words and illustrations below and use them in conjunction with the category title cards from page 17. Ask the children to sort the words as though they appear in some school books: which words could be found in a book about maths, which in a literacy book and which in a history book? Could any of the words appear in more than one of the books? Could any of the words appear in all three books? As an extension activity, ask the children to compose orally two or three sentences that feature some of the words they have discussed. They could write out the best sentences.

mathematics	calculation	kings	queens	Tudors
Vikings	invaders	settlers	evacuation	area
graph	product	fraction	increase	double
poem	story	essay	adjective	noun
verb	punctuation	division	approximately	pattern

Andrew Brodie: Improving Vocabulary for ages 8-9 © Bloomsbury Publishing Plc 2012

Word sorting:
maths, literacy, history

Name _____

Date _____

Teacher's notes

Discuss the words below in relation to the category title cards from page 17. Do the children know what each word means? Can they think of any related words? For example, they could suggest the word 'divide' in relation to the word 'division'. Ask the children to sort the words as though they appear in some non-fiction books: Could any of the words appear in more than one of the books? Could any of the words appear in all three books?

Word Bank

mathematics   kings   queens   area

Tudors   approximately   invaders

evacuation   settlers   fraction

graph   adjective   story   verb

ancient   comma

double   product   pattern   punctuation

poem

essay   paragraph   conquer   sentence   increase

noun

percentage   decimal   Vikings

division   sequence   battle   historical   calculation

Look carefully at the words in the Word Bank. Which words could be found in a book about maths, which in a book about literacy and which could be found in a book about history? Write the words in the correct places below. Some of the words could appear in more than one book.

Maths	**History**	*Literacy*

On a separate piece of paper, write three sentences using some of the vocabulary relating to maths, literacy and history.

Word sorting: maths, literacy, history

Name _____

Date _____

Teacher's notes

Discuss the words below in relation to the category title cards from page 17. Do the children know what each word means? To find extra vocabulary for each list, the children could research in the school library or on the internet. They could also consider searching for words related to those on the list: for example, the word 'punctuate' is clearly related to the word 'punctuation'.

Word Bank

adjective   queens   evacuation   kings   mathematics
calculation   division   invaders   Tudors   verb
noun   approximately
fraction   pattern   comma   paragraph   product   graph
punctuation   sentence   percentage   fiction   battle   settlers
ancient   estimation   conquerer   poem   area
Vikings   historical   twentieth   sequence   essay
conquer   factor   increase
double   decimal   remainder   story   consecutive

Look carefully at the words in the Word Bank. Write the words in the correct book below. Some of the words could appear in more than one book.

Maths	History	Literacy
_____ _____	_____ _____	_____ _____
_____ _____	_____ _____	_____ _____
_____ _____	_____ _____	_____ _____
_____ _____	_____ _____	_____ _____
_____ _____	_____ _____	_____ _____
_____ _____	_____ _____	_____ _____
_____ _____	_____ _____	_____ _____
_____ _____	_____ _____	_____ _____
_____ _____	_____ _____	_____ _____

Find some more vocabulary for each book.

Andrew Brodie: Improving Vocabulary for ages 8-9 © Bloomsbury Publishing Plc 2012

Word sorting: sea, country, city

Non-fiction

Information

Sea

Country

City

Teacher's notes

Photocopy and cut out the Non-fiction or Information headings and the category title cards to use in conjunction with the activities on the following three sheets. This type of categorisation activity can be very challenging for some children. It is important that they explain their choices when they are sorting the words - they may make some surprising decisions but ones that are perfectly valid.

Word sorting:
sea, country, city

Teacher's notes

Cut out the words and illustrations below and use them in conjunction with the category title cards from page 21. Ask the children to sort the words as though they appear in some school books: which words could be found in a book about the sea, which in a book about the country and which in a book about the city? Could any of the words appear in more than one of the books? Could any of the words appear in all three books? As an extension activity, ask the children to compose orally two or three sentences that feature some of the words they have discussed. They could write out the best sentences.

beach	waves	holiday	ocean	surf
gull	yacht	dolphin	lighthouse	agriculture
forest	moor	crops	animals	badger
river	hedge	taxi	centre	factory
museum	gallery	theatre	station	fox

Name _____

Date _____

Word sorting: sea, country, city

Teacher's notes

Discuss the words below in relation to the category title cards from page 21. Do the children know what each word means? Can they think of any related words? For example, they could suggest the word 'agricultural' in relation to the word 'agriculture'. Ask the children to sort the words as though they appear in some non-fiction books: Could any of the words appear in more than one of the books? Could any of the words appear in all three books?

Word Bank

waves beach gull environment marine depth

holiday pollution lighthouse

ocean moor lake aquatic

surf crops animals

yacht diving centre

ferry forest factory fern telescope

agriculture buildings

harvest dolphin taxi

tractor fox office cab

river museum theatre tram weasel

hedge station gallery badger liner

transport

Look carefully at the words in the Word Bank. Which words could be found in a book about the sea, which in a book about the country and which could be found in a book about the city? Write the words in the correct places below. Some of the words could appear in more than one book.

The Sea	*The Country*	**The City**

On a separate piece of paper, write three sentences using some of the vocabulary relating to the sea, the country or the city.

Word sorting: sea, country, city

Teacher's notes

Discuss the words below in relation to the category title cards from page 21. Do the children know what each word means? To find extra vocabulary for each list, the children could research in the school library or on the internet. They could also consider searching for words related to those on the list: for example, the word 'environmental' is clearly related to the word 'environment'.

Word Bank

beach   environment   waves   depth   yacht   ocean   hedge   liner

crops   forest   surf   fox   telescope   office   diving

gull   weasel   agriculture   schooner   badger

lighthouse   lake   cab

ferry   transport   remote   factory   tram

pollution   fern

moor   animals   river   submarine

station   lonely

mariner   harvest   aquatic   taxi   centre

gallery

tractor   museum   buildings

dolphin   marine   theatre   holiday   vehicle

Look carefully at the words in the Word Bank. Write the words in the correct book below. Some of the words could appear in more than one book.

The Sea		The Country	The City
_____	_____	_____	_____
_____	_____	_____	_____
_____	_____	_____	_____
_____	_____	_____	_____
_____	_____	_____	_____
_____	_____	_____	_____
_____	_____	_____	_____
_____	_____	_____	_____
_____	_____	_____	_____

Find some more vocabulary for each book.

Word sorting: vehicles, buildings, music

Non-fiction

Information

Vehicles

Buildings

Music

Teacher's notes

Photocopy and cut out the Non-fiction or Informaties headings buid the category title cards to use in conjunction with the activities on the following three sheets. This categorisation activity can be very challenging for some children. It is important that they explain their choices when they are sorting the words - they may make some surprising decisions but ones that are perfectly valid.

Word sorting: vehicles, buildings, music

Teacher's notes

Cut out the words and illustrations below and use them in conjunction with the category title cards from page 25. Ask the children to sort the words as though they appear in some school books: which words could be found in a book about vehicles, which in a book about buildings and which in a book about music? Could any of the words appear in more than one of the books? Could any of the words appear in all three books? As an extension activity, ask the children to compose orally two or three sentences that feature some of the words they have discussed. They could write out the best sentences.

		exterior	interior	
house	bungalow			flats
apartments	offices	bridge	car	lorry
bus	coach	van	hovercraft	motorcycle
train	wheels	piano	guitar	ukulele
recorder	organ	tune	melody	notes

Andrew Brodie: Improving Vocabulary for ages 8-9 © Bloomsbury Publishing Plc 2012

Word sorting: vehicles, buildings, music

Name _____

Date _____

Teacher's notes

Discuss the words below in relation to the category title cards from page 25. Do the children know what each word means? Can they think of any related words? For example, they could suggest the word 'external' in relation to the word 'exterior'. Ask the children to sort the words as though they appear in some non-fiction books: Could any of the words appear in more than one of the books? Could any of the words appear in all three books?

Word Bank

house   bridge   band   exterior   recorder   bungalow
interior   organ   offices   digger   orchestra
tuneful   foundations   melody   school
builder   guitar   lorry   scooter
crane   train   truck
musical   car   bicycle   van   wheels   factory
piano   tune   motorcycle   coach   hovercraft   construct
structure   notes   ukulele
apartments   bus   warehouse   flats   musician

Look carefully at the words in the Word Bank. Which words could be found in a book about vehicles, which in a book about buildings and which could be found in a book about music? Write the words in the correct places below. Some of the words could appear in more than one book.

Vehicles	Buildings	Music

On a separate piece of paper, write three sentences using some of the vocabulary relating to vehicles, buildings or music.

Word sorting:
vehicles, buildings, music

Teacher's notes

Discuss the words below in relation to the category title cards from page 25. Do the children know what each word means? To find extra vocabulary for each list, the children could research in the school library or on the internet. They could also consider searching for words related to those on the list: for example, the word 'incubation' is clearly related to the word 'incubate'.

Word Bank

house   tuneful   tune   van   piano
    bridge   crane   hovercraft   wheels   flats   structure
                        train
coach   organ   offices   musical   factory   scooter
                                                                                    notes
    bicycle   apartments   transportation   bus   foundations
        musician   melodious   digger   interior
                                            lorry   builder
warehouse   instrumental   exterior   school
    guitar   car   chassis   construct   melody
        truck   ukulele
                                    band
motorcycle   recorder   stairway   orchestra   bungalow

Look carefully at the words in the Word Bank. Write the words in the correct book below. Some of the words could appear in more than one book.

Vehicles	*Buildings*	**Music**

Find some more vocabulary for each book.

    Andrew Brodie: Improving Vocabulary for ages 8-9 © Bloomsbury Publishing Plc 2012

Winter

Nouns

Adjectives

Comparative adjectives

Teacher's notes

Photocopy and cut out these category title cards to use in conjunction with the activities on the following three sheets. This activity provides lots of opportunities for speaking and listening and introduces important everyday vocabulary.

Winter

Teacher's notes

Cut out the words and illustrations below and use them in conjunction with the category title cards from page 29. Use the cards created from this sheet as prompts for discussion to ensure that this is a speaking and listening activity as well as a reading task. Encourage the children to talk about what they remember of the winter. Can the children create oral sentences using some of the nouns and adjectives? Talk about the adjectives 'dark' and 'darker', explaining that 'darker' is called a comparative adjective because it compares the amount of darkness. Can the children find other comparative adjectives? Discuss the words 'frost' and 'frosty': the word 'frost' is a noun but 'frosty' is an adjective, which could be used in a phrase such as 'a frosty day' or 'a frosty morning' where the adjective is describing the nouns 'day' or 'morning'. After discussing the comparative adjectives, ask the children to create some more oral sentences now using some of these.

season	winter	December	January	February
day	night	morning	evening	dark
darker	cold	colder	freezing	frozen
frost	frosty	snow	snowy	snowier
snowdrift	ice	icicle	icy	icier

Andrew Brodie: Improving Vocabulary for ages 8-9 © Bloomsbury Publishing Plc 2012

Winter

Teacher's notes

Discuss the words in the Word Bank in conjunction with the category title cards from page 29. Ensure that this is firstly a speaking and listening activity although it will provide practice in both reading and writing. Encourage the children to talk about what they remember of the winter. Can the children create oral sentences using some of the nouns and adjectives? Note the inclusion of the word 'biting' as an adjective. Talk about the adjectives 'dark' and 'darker', explaining that 'darker' is called a comparative adjective because it compares the amount of darkness. Discuss the words 'frost' and 'frosty': the word 'frost' is a noun but 'frosty' is an adjective, which could be used in a phrase such as 'a frosty day' or 'a frosty morning' where the adjective is describing the nouns 'day' or 'morning'. Do the children recognise the comparative adjective that has been created from the adjective 'frosty'? After discussing the comparative adjectives, ask the children to create some more oral sentences now using some of these.

Word Bank

season   dark   snowy   January   winter
frozen   cold   icicle
frostier   freezing   day   ice   evening   deeper
icy   snowdrift   morning   rain
rainy   night   earlier   seasonal   late
deep   early   dawn   rainier   dusk   snow
biting   colder   darker
snowier   February
December   frosty   later   frost
icier

Write the words from the Word Bank in the appropriate places in the table.

Nouns	Adjectives

On a separate piece of paper, write three brilliant sentences describing the winter.

Winter

Name _____

Date _____

Teacher's notes

Discuss the words in the Word Bank in conjunction with the category title cards from page 29. Ensure that this is firstly a speaking and listening activity although it will provide practice in both reading and writing. Encourage the children to talk about what they remember of the winter. Can the children create oral sentences using some of the nouns and adjectives? Talk about the adjectives 'cold' and 'colder', explaining that 'colder' is called a comparative adjective because it compares the amount of coldness. Discuss the words 'snow' and 'snowy': the word 'snow' is a noun but 'snowy' is an adjective, which could be used in a phrase such as 'a snowy day' where the adjective is describing the noun 'day'. Do the children recognise the comparative adjective that has been created from the adjective 'snowy'? After discussing the comparative adjectives, ask the children to create some more oral sentences now using some of these.

Word Bank

season   December
winter   evening   darker   icy
January   frozen   frost
cold   dark   rainy   seasonal   rain   deep
icicle   biting   colder
freezing   ice   frostier
snow   early   frosty
snowier   late   February   dawn   snowy   earlier
day   deeper   night   icier
snowdrift   dusk   morning   later   rainier

Write the adjectives from the Word Bank in the appropriate places in the table. One set of adjectives has already been written in the table. Two sets of comparative adjectives need to be completed. Can you think of extra words to write in the table?

Adjectives	
dark	darker
chilly	
fierce	

On a separate piece of paper, write three brilliant sentences describing the winter.

Andrew Brodie: Improving Vocabulary for ages 8-9 © Bloomsbury Publishing Plc 2012

Spring

Spring

Nouns

Adjectives

Comparative adjectives

Teacher's notes

Photocopy and cut out the Spring heading and the other category title cards to use in conjunction with the activities on the following three sheets. This activity provides lots of opportunities for speaking and listening and introduces important everyday vocabulary.

Spring

Teacher's notes

Cut out the words and illustrations below and use them in conjunction with the category title cards from page 33. Use the cards created from this sheet as prompts for discussion to ensure that this is a speaking and listening activity rather than a reading activity. Encourage the children to talk about what they remember of the spring. Can the children create oral sentences using some of the nouns and adjectives? Talk about the adjectives 'warm' and 'warmer', explaining that 'warmer' is called a comparative adjective because it compares the amount of warmth. Can the children find other comparative adjectives? Do the children understand the term 'mild'? After discussing the comparative adjectives, ask the children to create some more oral sentences now using some of these.

season	spring	March	April	May
evenings	light	lighter	bright	brighter
flowers	daffodils	blossom	eggs	birds
nests	leaves	trees	hedges	warm
warmer	mild	milder	temperature	green

Andrew Brodie: Improving Vocabulary for ages 8-9 © Bloomsbury Publishing Plc 2012

Spring

Teacher's notes

Discuss the words in the Word Bank in conjunction with the category title cards from page 33. Ensure that this is firstly a speaking and listening activity although it will provide practice in both reading and writing. Encourage the children to talk about what they remember of the spring. Can the children create oral sentences using some of the nouns and adjectives? Talk about the adjectives 'light' and 'lighter', explaining that 'lighter' is called a comparative adjective because it compares the amount of light. Can the children find other comparative adjectives? Do the children understand the term 'mild'? Discuss the words 'rain' and 'rainy': the word 'rain' is a noun but 'rainy' is an adjective, which could be used in a phrase such as 'a rainy afternoon' where the adjective is describing the noun 'afternoon'. Do the children recognise both adjectives that have been created from the noun 'rain' (rainy, rainier)? After discussing the comparative adjectives, ask the children to create some more oral sentences now using some of these.

Word Bank

season light April spring nests flowers warm March evenings
eggs mild trees rain bright blossom leaves brighter
lighter temperature hedges buds daytime milder
mistier sunshine
green wet springlike
daffodils rainier night-time birds
warmer misty greener rainy shoots
wetter May

Write the words from the Word Bank in the appropriate places in the table.

Nouns	Adjectives

On a separate piece of paper, write three super sentences describing the spring.

Spring

Teacher's notes

Discuss the words in the Word Bank in conjunction with the category title cards from page 33. Ensure that this is firstly a speaking and listening activity although it will provide practice in both reading and writing. Encourage the children to talk about what they remember of the spring. Talk about the adjectives 'bright' and 'brighter', explaining that 'brighter' is called a comparative adjective because it compares the amount of brightness. Can the children find other comparative adjectives? Do the children understand the term 'mild'? Discuss the words 'mist' and 'misty': the word 'mist' is a noun but 'misty' is an adjective, which could be used in a phrase such as 'a misty morning' where the adjective is describing the noun 'morning'. Do the children recognise both adjectives that have been created from the noun 'mist' (misty, mistier)? After discussing the comparative adjectives, ask the children to create some more oral sentences now using some of these. Note that the adjective 'springlike' cannot be extended to create comparative adjectives without adding the words 'more' or 'most'.

Word Bank

season light April spring nests flowers warm March evenings

eggs mild trees rain bright blossom leaves brighter

lighter temperature hedges buds daytime milder

green mistier sunshine wet birds springlike

daffodils rainier night-time rainy shoots

warmer misty wetter greener May

Write the adjectives from the Word Bank in the appropriate places in the table. One set of adjectives has already been written in the table. Can you think of extra words to write in the table?

Adjectives	
warm	**warmer**

On a separate piece of paper, write three super sentences describing the spring.

Andrew Brodie: Improving Vocabulary for ages 8-9 © Bloomsbury Publishing Plc 2012

Summer

Summer

Nouns

Adjectives

Comparative adjectives

Teacher's notes

Photocopy and cut out these category title cards to use in conjunction with the activities on the following three sheets. This activity provides lots of opportunities for speaking and listening and introduces important everyday vocabulary.

Summer

Teacher's notes

Cut out the words and illustrations below and use them in conjunction with the category title cards from page 37. Use the cards created from this sheet as prompts for discussion to ensure that this is a speaking and listening activity rather than a reading activity. Encourage the children to talk about what they remember of the summer. Can the children create oral sentences using some of the nouns and adjectives? The children should now be familiar with comparative adjectives. Can they find the comparative adjectives? After discussing the comparative adjectives, ask the children to create some more oral sentences using some of these.

season	summer	June	July	August
holidays	sunshine	sunny	sunnier	light
lighter	evenings	outside	hot	hotter
sweltering	heat	seaside	beach	countryside
field	trees	shade	shady	shadier

Andrew Brodie: Improving Vocabulary for ages 8-9 © Bloomsbury Publishing Plc 2012

Summer

Name _____

Date _____

Teacher's notes

Discuss the words in the Word Bank in conjunction with the category title cards from page 37. Ensure that this is firstly a speaking and listening activity although it will provide practice in both reading and writing. Encourage the children to talk about what they remember of the summer. Can the children create oral sentences using some of the nouns and adjectives? Can they find the comparative adjectives? You may wish to take the opportunity to point out how the letter y is replaced by an i when the word sunny is changed to sunnier. Discuss the adjective enjoyable: how could this be used in a sentence about summer? How could comparisons be made using this adjective? Hopefully the children will see the need to insert the word 'more' to be able to say 'more enjoyable'.

Word Bank

season   July   outside   light   August

June   holidays   sunny   summer   bluer

sweltering   swifts   beach   grassier
                                        trees   hotter   shade

hot   grassy   sky   starry   shady   sunshine

blistering   enjoyable   evenings

field   field   countryside   swallows
    lighter   starrier   heat

blue   sunnier

seaside   star   grass   enjoyment

Write the words from the Word Bank in the appropriate places in the table.

Nouns	Adjectives

On a separate piece of paper, write three sentences describing the summer.

Andrew Brodie: Improving Vocabulary for ages 8-9 © Bloomsbury Publishing Plc 2012

Summer

Teacher's notes

Discuss the words in the Word Bank in conjunction with the category title cards from page 37. Ensure that this is firstly a speaking and listening activity although it will provide practice in both reading and writing. Encourage the children to talk about what they remember of the summer. Can they find the comparative adjectives in the Word Bank? You may wish to take the opportunity to point out how the letter y is replaced by an i when the word grassy is changed to grassier. Discuss the adjective relaxing: how could this be used in a sentence about summer? How could comparisons be made using this adjective? Hopefully the children will see the need to insert the word 'more' to be able to say 'more relaxing'. Note that some children may state that relaxing is a verb, which is correct in phrases such as 'I was relaxing on the beach' but here we are using it as an adjective as in 'it was a very relaxing day'.

Word Bank

season   July   outside   light   August

June   holidays   sunny   summer   bluer

sweltering   swifts   beach   grassier   shade

grassy   sky   starry   trees   hotter

hot   enjoyable   evenings   shady   sunshine

blistering

field   field   relaxing   countryside   swallows

lighter   starrier   heat

blue   seaside   star   grass   sunnier   enjoyment

Write the adjectives from the Word Bank in the appropriate places in the table. Two sets of adjectives have already been written in the table. Can you think of extra words to write in the table?

Adjectives	
sunny	sunnier
enjoyable	more enjoyable

On a separate piece of paper, write four sentences describing the summer.

    Andrew Brodie: Improving Vocabulary for ages 8-9 © Bloomsbury Publishing Plc 2012

Autumn

Autumn

Nouns

Adjectives

Comparative adjectives

Verbs

Teacher's notes

Photocopy and cut out these category title cards to use in conjunction with the activities on the following three sheets. Note that the word category 'verbs' is reintroduced in this Key Activity.

Autumn

Teacher's notes

Cut out the words and illustrations below and use them in conjunction with the category title cards from page 41. Use the cards created from this sheet as prompts for discussion to ensure that this is a speaking and listening activity rather than a reading activity. Encourage the children to talk about what they remember of the autumn. Note that, unlike the lists for the other seasons, this set of words contains some verbs - can the children identify them? Can they create oral sentences using some of the nouns, verbs and adjectives? Can they find the comparative adjectives?

season	autumn	September	October	November
wind	blowy	blowier	leaves	golden
brown	orange	damp	damper	fog
foggy	foggier	blowing	falling	rolling
running	tumbling	storm	stormy	stormier

Andrew Brodie: Improving Vocabulary for ages 8-9 © Bloomsbury Publishing Plc 2012

Autumn

Name _____

Date _____

Teacher's notes

Discuss the words in the Word Bank in conjunction with the category title cards from page 41. Ensure that this is firstly a speaking and listening activity although it will provide practice in both reading and writing. Encourage the children to talk about what they remember of the autumn. Note that, unlike the lists for the other seasons, this set of words contains some verbs - can the children identify them? Can they notice the two verb forms of 'to gather', ie 'gathering' and 'gathered'? Ask them to create an oral sentence for each of these. Can they find the comparative adjectives?

Word Bank

season   blowier   orange   blowy   rolling   October

autumn   windswept

wind   hurricane   damper   harvesting

golden   fog   migrating   storm   blustery

departing

damp   blowing   September   gale   gathering   brown

foggier   falling

leaves   birds   harvest   stormier   autumnal

harvested   running

November   wrapped   stormy   tumbling   gathered   foggy

Write the words from the Word Bank in the appropriate places in the table.

Nouns	Verbs	Adjectives

Autumn

Name _____

Date _____

Teacher's notes

Discuss the words in the Word Bank in conjunction with the category title cards from page 41. Ensure that this is firstly a speaking and listening activity although it will provide practice in both reading and writing. Encourage the children to talk about what they remember of the autumn. Note that, unlike the lists for the other seasons, this set of words contains some verbs - can the children identify them? Can they notice the two verb forms of 'to gather', ie 'gathering' and 'gathered'? Ask them to create an oral sentence for each of these. Can they find the comparative adjectives?

Word Bank

season shaking blowier dense windswept blowy shivering October
autumn dark harvesting
fierce golden fog hurricane engulfing migrating damper storm blustery
departing blowing September trembling gathering ferocious
damp foggier falling darkness tugging autumnal running
gale harvested leaves birds harvest stormier
November wrapped stormy tumbling gathered foggy rolling

Write the words from the Word Bank in the appropriate places in the table.
Can you think of extra words to write in the table?

Nouns	Verbs	Adjectives

Word sorting: castles, trees, flowers

Non-fiction

Information

Castles

Trees

Flowers

Teacher's notes

Photocopy and cut out the Non-fiction or Information headings and the category title cards to use in conjunction with the activities on the following three sheets. This categorisation activity can be very challenging for some children. It is important that they explain their choices when they are sorting the words - they may make some surprising decisions but ones that are perfectly valid.

Word sorting: castles, trees, flowers

Teacher's notes

Cut out the words and illustrations below and use them in conjunction with the category title cards from page 45. Ask the children to sort the words as though they appear in some non-fiction books: which words could be found in a book about castles, which in a book about trees and which could be found in a book about flowers? Could any of the words appear in more than one of the books? Could any of the words appear in all three books? As an extension activity, ask the children to compose orally two or three sentences that feature some of the words they have discussed. They could write out the best sentences.

castle	tree	flower	petal	blossom
stem	trunk	moat	portcullis	defence
protection	protect	tower	tall	strong
strength	stronger	strongest	leaf	leaves
beautiful	guarded	branch	evergreen	roots

Andrew Brodie: Improving Vocabulary for ages 8-9 © Bloomsbury Publishing Plc 2012

Name _____

Date _____

Word sorting: castles, trees, flowers

Teacher's notes

Discuss the words below in relation to the category title cards from page 45. Do the children know what each word means? Can they think of any related words? For example, they could suggest the word 'fortification' in relation to the word 'fortified'. Ask the children to sort the words as though they appear in some non-fiction books: Could any of the words appear in more than one of the books? Could any of the words appear in all three books?

Word Bank

castle   flower   tower   defence   petal   stem   protect

moat   tree   stronger   beech   blossom   fort

protection   roots   oak   rose

strong   portcullis   beautiful   evergreen

leaves   keep   fortified   pine   knight   daffodil   drawbridge

guarded   bark   crown   tall   strongest

trunk   branch   strength   battlements   leaf   soldier

Look carefully at the words in the Word Bank. Which words could be found in a book about castles, which in a book about trees and which could be found in a book about flowers? Write the words in the correct places below. Some of the words could appear in more than one book. You may like to add some extra words.

Castles	*Trees*	**Flowers**

On a separate piece of paper, write three sentences using some of the vocabulary relating to castles, trees or flowers.

Word sorting: castles, trees, flowers

Name _____

Date _____

Teacher's notes

Discuss the words below in relation to the category title cards from page 45. Do the children know what each word means? To find extra vocabulary for each list, the children could research in the school library or on the internet. They could also consider searching for words related to those on the list: for example, the word 'defensive' is clearly related to the word 'defence'.

Word Bank

castle   flower   tower   defence   petal   blossom   protect

tree   moat   protection   stronger   beech   soldier   fort

tall   evergreen   portcullis   oak   guarded   rose

leaves   keep   fortified   knight   deciduous   daffodil   conifer

beautiful   bark   pine   inhabitants   drawbridge

crown   broad-leaved   courageous

impregnable   strong   strongest

trunk   branch   strength   battlements   roots   stem   leaf

Look carefully at the words in the Word Bank. Write the words in the correct book below. Some of the words could appear in more than one book.

Castles	*Trees*	**Flowers**

Find some more vocabulary for each book.

Andrew Brodie: Improving Vocabulary for ages 8-9 © Bloomsbury Publishing Plc 2012

Word sorting: atlas, weather, electricity

Non-fiction

Information

Atlas

Weather

Electricity

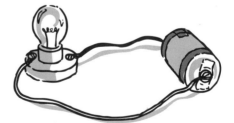

Teacher's notes

Photocopy and cut out the Non-fiction or Information headings and the category title cards to use in conjunction with the activities on the following three sheets. This categorisation activity can be very challenging for some children. It is important that they explain their choices when they are sorting the words - they may make some surprising decisions but ones that are perfectly valid.

Word sorting:
atlas, weather, electricity

Teacher's notes

Cut out the words and illustrations below and use them in conjunction with the category title cards from page 49. Ask the children to sort the words as though they appear in some non-fiction books: which words could be found in an atlas, which in a book about weather and which could be found in a book about electricity? Could any of the words appear in more than one of the books? Could any of the words appear in all three books? As an extension activity, ask the children to compose orally two or three sentences that feature some of the words they have discussed. They could write out the best sentences.

map	globe	continent	country	mountain
river	ocean	sea	temperature	thermometer
cloud	high pressure	low pressure	climate	seasonal
circuit	electrical	current	wire	battery
bulb	flow	electricity	desert	forest

Andrew Brodie: Improving Vocabulary for ages 8-9 © Bloomsbury Publishing Plc 2012

Word sorting: atlas, weather, electricity

Teacher's notes

Discuss the words below in relation to the category title cards from page 49. Do the children know what each word means? Can they think of any related words? For example, they could suggest the word 'continental' in relation to the word 'continent'. You may like to suggest that the children look in an atlas - they may be surprised to find that there is more information than just maps. Ask the children to sort the words as though they appear in some non-fiction books: Could any of the words appear in more than one of the books? Could any of the words appear in all three books?

Word Bank

map	temperature	bulb	continent	country	battery
river	seasonal	current	shock	forest	thermometer
cloud	cold front	circuit	climate		warm front
high pressure	flow	globe	population	wire
	sea	desert	geology		ocean
mountain	switch	low pressure	electricity
agriculture	electrical		

Look carefully at the words in the Word Bank. Which words could be found in an atlas, which in a book about weather and which could be found in a book about electricity? Write the words in the correct places below. Some of the words could appear in more than one book. You may like to add some extra words.

Atlas	*Weather*	**Electricity**
___ ___	___ ___	___ ___
___ ___	___ ___	___ ___
___ ___	___ ___	___ ___
___ ___	___ ___	___ ___
___ ___	___ ___	___ ___
___ ___	___ ___	___ ___
___ ___	___ ___	___ ___

On a separate piece of paper, write three sentences using some of the vocabulary relating to an atlas, weather or electricity.

Word sorting: atlas, weather, electricity

Name _____

Date _____

Teacher's notes

Discuss the words below in relation to the category title cards from page 49. Do the children know what each word means? To find extra vocabulary for each list, the children could research in the school library or on the internet. They could also consider searching for words related to those on the list: for example, the word 'climatic' is clearly related to the word 'climate'.

Word Bank

map   temperature   continent   country   battery

river   seasonal   current   shock   forest   thermometer

precipitation

cloud   cold front   globe   climate   warm front

flow

high pressure   desert   population   wire   tropical

bulb   sea   hurricane   geology   hydro-electric   ocean

mountain   generating   low pressure   electricity

circuit   agriculture   electrical   switch

Look carefully at the words in the Word Bank. Write the words in the correct book below. Some of the words could appear in more than one book.

Atlas	*Weather*	**Electricity**

Find some more specialist vocabulary for each book.

Andrew Brodie: Improving Vocabulary for ages 8-9 © Bloomsbury Publishing Plc 2012

Word sorting: furniture, clothing, books

Non-fiction

Information

Furniture

Clothing

Books

Teacher's notes

Photocopy and cut out the Non-fiction or Information headings and the category title cards to use in conjunction with the activities on the following three sheets. This categorisation activity can be very challenging for some children. It is important that they explain their choices when they are sorting the words - they may make some surprising decisions but ones that are perfectly valid.

Word sorting: furniture, clothing, books

Teacher's notes

Cut out the words and illustrations below and use them in conjunction with the category title cards from page 53. Ask the children to sort the words as though they appear in some catalogues: which words could be found in a furniture catalogue, which in a clothing catalogue and which could be found in a books catalogue? Do they feel that any of the words are not suitable for any of the catalogues? Are any of the words synonyms? Could any of the words appear in more than one of the catalogues? As an extension activity, ask the children to compose orally two or three sentences that feature some of the words they have discussed. They could write out the best sentences.

trousers	shirt	jumper	pullover	jersey
vest	sandals	cardigan	table	chair
sideboard	wardrobe	sofa	settee	lounge
bedroom	stool	dictionary	atlas	picture book
diary	poetry	drama	tables	fiction

Andrew Brodie: Improving Vocabulary for ages 8-9 © Bloomsbury Publishing Plc 2012

Word sorting: furniture, clothing, books

Name _____

Date _____

Teacher's notes

Discuss the words below in relation to the category title cards from page 53. Do the children know what each word means? Can they think of any related words? For example, they could suggest the word 'sweatshirt' in relation to the word 'shirt'. Which words could be found in a furniture catalogue, which in a clothing catalogue and which could be found in a books catalogue? Do they feel that any of the words are not suitable for any of the catalogues? Are any of the words synonyms? Could any of the words appear in more than one of the catalogues? Are the children familiar with skorts? Can they tell which two names for clothing items have been combined to create this new word? Do they know which two names for clothing items have been combined to create the new word jeggings?

Word Bank

skirt   jersey   leggings   illustrator   science   shorts   shirt
jumper   fiction   author   travel
chair   publisher   pullover   stool   price   poetry
classic   cabinet   bookshelves   times   settee   dictionary
atlas   sandals   table   cardigan   bedroom   trousers
diary   drama   vest   reference
nature   lounge   desk   wardrobe   sideboard   tables   sofa
picture book

Look carefully at the words in the Word Bank. Which words could be found in a furniture catalogue, which in a clothing catalogue and which could be found in a books catalogue? Write the words in the correct places below. Some of the words could appear in more than one book. You may like to add some extra words.

Furniture	Clothing	Books

On a separate piece of paper, write three sentences using some of the vocabulary that could be found in a furniture catalogue, a clothing catalogue and a books catalogue.

Word sorting: furniture, clothing, books

Teacher's notes

Discuss the words below in relation to the category title cards from page 53. Which words could be found in a furniture catalogue, which in a clothing catalogue and which could be found in a books catalogue? Do they feel that any of the words are not suitable for any of the catalogues? Are any of the words synonyms? Could any of the words appear in more than one of the catalogues? Are the children familiar with skorts? Can they tell which two names for clothing items have been combined to create this new word? Do they know which two names for clothing items have been combined to create the new word jeggings?

Word Bank

skirt jersey leggings illustrator science linen shorts shirt

jumper fiction author contents travel

denim chair publisher pullover foam stool price

classic cabinet bookshelves times settee polyester

atlas beech bedroom dictionary

cardigan sandals introduction table vest trousers cotton

oak diary tables reference

nature drama sideboard

pages lounge desk wardrobe picture book sofa poetry

Look carefully at the words in the Word Bank. Write the words in the correct catalogue below. Some of the words could appear in more than one catalogue.

Furniture	Clothing	Books

Find some more specialist vocabulary for each catalogue.

Skills and talents

Skills and talents

Verbs

Nouns

Adverbs

Kyra dances beautifully.

Ben plays football brilliantly.

Teacher's notes

Photocopy and cut out these category title cards to use in conjunction with the activities on the following three sheets. This activity introduces a range of adverbs. Note that grammatical terms such 'adverbs' and 'adjectives' are in themselves useful vocabulary for the pupils.

Skills and talents

Teacher's notes

Cut out the words and illustrations below and use them in conjunction with the category title cards from page 57. Use the cards created from this sheet as prompts for discussion to ensure that this is a speaking and listening activity rather than a reading activity. Encourage the children to talk about skills or talents that they have or that someone they know has. If these are not shown on the cards, you may wish to add them. Show the children the two short sentences: 'Kyra dances beautifully' and 'Ben plays football brilliantly'. Ask them to create some similar short sentences using each of the name cards together with a verb, an adverb and, if necessary, a noun. They do not have to write the sentences but could do so as an extension activity.

Kyra	Ben	Jasdeep	Tom	Esme
Tariq	performs	dances	acts	plays
writes	sings	gymnastics	drama	football
songs	trampolining	guitar	beautifully	brilliantly
wonderfully	fantastically	incredibly	amazingly	

Andrew Brodie: Improving Vocabulary for ages 8-9 © Bloomsbury Publishing Plc 2012